STEAM

PORTRAITS
1960–1966

This book is dedicated to my parents for their patience and to my wife for her assistance in copy and proof reading.

STEAM
PORTRAITS
1960–1966

BRIAN J. DICKSON

ALAN SUTTON PUBLISHING LIMITED

First Published in the United Kingdom in 1994
Alan Sutton Publishing Limited
Phoenix Mill · Far Thrupp · Stroud · Gloucestershire

First published in the United States of America in 1994
Alan Sutton Publishing Inc.
83 Washington Street · Dover · NH 03820

British Library Cataloguing-in-Publication Data

A catalogue record for this book is available from the British Library.

ISBN 0-7509-0750-9

Library of Congress Cataloging-in-Publication Data applied for.

Typeset in 11/12 Times.
Typesetting and origination by
Alan Sutton Publishing Limited.
Printed in Great Britain by
Butler & Tanner, Frome, Somerset.

Introduction

This book has come together almost by accident after the rediscovery of a box of photographic negatives which I had taken during the early 1960s. They had accumulated over these years as a result of travelling around Britain following steam locomotives to most regions. The bulk of them had never been printed photographically until the idea for the book grew in 1992 and what started as a random trawl through the negatives became a systematic search for good and interesting pictures.

This selection of photographs was taken over a period of six years which saw the demise of the steam locomotive as the prime motive power for British Railways. They record working locomotives throughout Britain and those at the end of their working life awaiting the scrapyard, showing engines with gleaming paintwork and those with the grime from years of neglect.

Living in Edinburgh gave me the opportunity to travel behind steam to most of the cities and towns in Scotland where a large number of steam locomotives still worked everything from express passenger to freight and branch line duties. In the early 1960s Waverley station in Edinburgh still had regular steam-hauled expresses to and from London with motive power coming from the two large depots in the city at Haymarket and St Margarets. The daily departure and arrival of the 'Elizabethan' behind an 'A4' was a joy to watch.

Journeys north were always fruitful, Aberdeen had Ferryhill and Kittybrewster depots, the latter having a fair number of stored locomotives due to the dieselization of the line to Inverness and the north. Every morning at Kittybrewster depot it was possible to see the overnight mail coaches from London being turned on the turntable in preparation for the return journey later that day and with the huge fishing fleet working out of the harbour, fish trains to London were still a regular daily duty. It was still possible to travel regularly behind Gresley 'A4' Pacifics between Aberdeen and Glasgow to tightly run schedules, and a lot of the traffic on the main lines from Perth and Glasgow south to England was still steam hauled with the wonderful northbound journey up Beattock being an exhilarating experience never to be forgotten.

The Glasgow depots of Polmadie, St Rollox and Corkerhill were regularly visited, Polmadie being the largest always had a wide range of locomotives from ex-LMS and LNER to Standard Pacifics still used on express passenger trains. At St Rollox there were always a few engines fresh from an overhaul at the works and at Corkerhill the depot staff must have taken a lot of pride in the locomotives stabled there as they always seemed to be very clean. Unfortunately other depots in the Glasgow area such as Dawsholm and Kipps had become the storage areas for large numbers of small freight and tank locomotives superseded by diesels. At Dawsholm it was possible to see the preserved ex-CR 4–2–2 No. 123 in store. Also there in a grim state was the ex-HR 4–4–0 No. 54398 *Ben Alder* awaiting a decision about preservation; unfortunately this never took place and the locomotive was scrapped.

In 1963 the Scottish Region of British Railways ran special passenger trains throughout Scotland behind the four preserved locomotives they then had: ex-GNSR 4–4–0 No. 49 *Gordon Highlander*, ex-NBR 4–4–0 No. 256 *Glen Douglas*, ex-CR 4–2–2 No. 123 and ex-HR 4–6–0 No. 103. These proved to be very successful with both railway enthusiasts and the public.

The Scottish region also had a wealth of branch lines, still steam worked, that were a joy to visit. The line from Thornton junction to Crail wandered up the Fife coast through picturesque fishing villages, a beautiful journey with lovely stations.

There was also a wealth of industrial lines to visit. These were run by various organizations, the National Coal Board being the largest. Brick works, gasworks, aluminium and steel works all had steam locomotives, some performing hard working duties. One of the largest was the Wemyss Private Railway in Fife serving coalmines and docks in the Wemyss, Leven and Methil area, transporting large amounts of coal to the loading staithes in Methil docks. Virtually all had depots where locomotives were both stabled and sometimes major as well as minor repairs were carried out.

Many annual holidays were spent travelling south to visit depots and lines that were still steam operated. Chester had a wonderful station with masses of steam traffic heading to and from the North Wales coast. Exeter still had steam workings in and around the area, but there were many signs of change, diesel workings were becoming more common on passenger trains, the 'Atlantic Coast Express' had become diesel hauled and many branch and local workings had become dieselized. This together with the increasing rate of line closures became the pattern during the mid-1960s with steam workings becoming rarer and opportunities for photography becoming more remote. A number of the photographs in the book show locomotives which have since been preserved, giving a glimpse of the engines during their working life.

The camera used was an Agfa 2¼ in square format with a maximum shutter speed of 1/250 of a second. All the photographs were catalogued with the date and location, a unique record of this period.

The West Highland line to Mallaig was still steam hauled in August 1960 with both ex-LNER and ex-LMS locomotives sharing the workload. One of the workhorses specifically designed by Sir Nigel Gresley for this line and introduced in 1937, 'K4' 2–6–0 No. 61997 *McCailin Mor*, has been coaled up and is now taking water before resting between duties at Fort William depot. Fortunately one of this class has been preserved, No. 61994 *The Great Marquess*, which is based at the Severn Valley Railway.

2 August 1960

St Margarets depot (64A) in Edinburgh was the largest in the city, supplying the bulk of the motive power for the old LNER routes radiating from Waverley station in the centre of the city. Haymarket depot (64B) on the opposite side of the city supplied the motive power for all the express passenger trains on the East Coast main line heading north to Aberdeen or south to London. On this day, ex-LNER 'A1' 4–6–2 No. 60115 *Meg Merrilies* sits over the ashpits at St Margarets.

7 August 1960

Princes Street station, Edinburgh, was the terminus for the Caledonian Railway line from Carstairs junction where it joined the main West Coast line to Carlisle and the south. Lines from here also served Glasgow via Shotts, Stirling and the north, branch lines in the area and a suburban line to Leith. Ex-LMS '4MT' 2–6–4 tank No. 42204 leaves the station for the carriage sidings; this engine was one of the Fairburn developments of a Stanier design. The shed code (66E) shows the locomotive was allocated to Carstairs depot.

2 July 1961

Standard '2MT' 2–6–2 tank No. 84006 has just backed into a bay platform at Northampton Castle station and the fireman is about to turn on the water to fill the tanks.

17 July 1961

Ex-CR '3F' 0–6–0 No. 57550 simmers quietly at the head of an enthusiasts' special in Leith North station. It had worked tender first from Edinburgh Princes Street station with the special and is now ready to take the train on to further branch lines in the Edinburgh area. This locomotive was from a McIntosh design introduced in 1899 and one of this class, No. 57566, has been preserved and is based at the Strathspey Railway. The Leith North branch was closed in April 1962.

3 February 1962

Two differing types of LMS 0–6–0 tanks. *Above* is '3F' 'Jinty' No. 47408 on shunting duties at Carlisle station on 24 March 1962. *Right,* '2F' No. 47168 in store at Hamilton depot on 22 April 1962. This class had a shorter wheelbase than the 'Jinty' and was used almost exclusively for dockyard work. Several examples of the 'Jinty' '3F' have been preserved.

A typical GWR scene? In fact, this was ex-Highland Railway territory at Dingwall. Sitting quietly in the bay platform is '1600' class 0–6–0 pannier tank No. 1649 while a milk van is unloaded. This engine was one of a pair sent north in 1957 to work the Dornoch branch after the two very old Drummond Highland 0–4–4 tanks were withdrawn. The Dornoch branch was closed to passenger traffic in June 1960 but the locomotives continued to work light freight around the area. The shed code plate (60C) indicates that the locomotive was allocated to Helmsdale depot. One of this class has been preserved at the Kent and East Sussex Railway.

9 July 1962

Ex-NER 'Q6' 0–8–0 No. 63432 reverses into West Hartlepool shed. This class was a Raven design introduced in 1913 and served all over north-east England on heavy freight traffic. Again, fortunately one of this class has been preserved as part of the National Railway Museum collection.
29 July 1962

Duddingston station was on the Edinburgh suburban Inner and Outer Circles and saw plenty of freight traffic heading round Edinburgh to the various goods yards in the city. Duddingston yard itself served the many breweries surrounding the station. *Above,* Standard '4MT' 2–6–0 No. 76105 is heading east with a freight train. *Right,* ex-NBR 'J37' 0–6–0 No. 64612 also heads east with a freight train. Both were probably making for the Millerhill marshalling yard on the southern edge of the city.

25 August 1962

Enthusiasts' special workings were becoming commonplace during the early 1960s and the Edinburgh area was no exception. On this day a special was working over many of the branch lines around the city and it arrived at Duddingston station behind a 'V3' tank locomotive. The photograph *above* was taken on the footplate of ex-NBR 'J35' 0–6–0 No. 64510 as it waited to propel the special up the steep bank from Duddingston yard to St Leonards goods yard in the city. *Right*, with a full head of steam, the engine starts to put some power behind its load as it hits the bottom of the bank.

25 August 1962

Left, having waited in Duddingston yard while the special was worked up to St Leonards and back, ex-LNER 'V3' 2–6–2 tank No. 67668 has now coupled up and is ready to work on to other branch lines in the area. Classes 'V1' and 'V3' were common in the Edinburgh area, being worked on the Inner and Outer Circle suburban trains until dieselization. *Above*, on the same day Standard '4MT' 2–6–0 No. 76105 is heading westbound through Duddingston station with a mixed freight.

25 August 1962

Thornton junction sat within the huge Fife coalfield and in consequence saw large amounts of coal traffic to the cities, towns, ports and power stations around the Firth of Forth. *Above*, ex-LNER 'J38' 0–6–0 No. 65901 passes the pit opposite Thornton junction depot with a coal train heading west towards Dunfermline. *Right*, sister engine No. 65902 is also heading west with a mixed freight. These locomotives were a Gresley design introduced in 1926 specifically for this type of traffic in Scotland.

15 September 1962

Standard '4MT' 2–6–4 tank No. 80122 sits over the ashpits at St Margarets depot in Edinburgh.
7 October 1962

Ex-CR '3F' 0–6–0 No. 57654 in store at Dalry Road depot in Edinburgh. The tender is empty and the front coupling has been removed. This Pickersgill designed locomotive was introduced in 1918 and is seen here at the end of its useful life.

13 October 1962

Standard '4MT' 2–6–4 tank No. 80022 puts its weight behind a train of empty coaching stock it is banking from Craigentinny yard, heading up the hill between St Margarets depot and Edinburgh Waverley station.

3 November 1962

A comparison between two ex-LNER 'A3' 4–6–2 locomotives at rest in Haymarket depot, Edinburgh. The engine on the right is No. 60053 *Sansovino*. On the left is No. 60088 *Book Law* wearing German-style smoke deflectors which give it a blinkered look.

11 November 1962

Standard '4MT' 2–6–4 tank No. 80006 coasts into Edinburgh Waverley station with a parcels train. The recess on the cab side of some of these locomotives shows the position for the automatic tablet catching gear used on some single line workings.

26 January 1963

Ex-LMS '7P' 'Royal Scot' 4–6–0 No. 46157 *The Royal Artilleryman* arriving at Edinburgh Waverley station leaking from every gland and making very heavy going at the head of a special train carrying rugby supporters from South Wales.

1 February 1963

Ex-LNER 'A3' 4–6–2 No. 60075 *St Frusquin* waits to pull away from Portobello station at the head of the Saturday-only, three-coach Berwick slow from Edinburgh Waverley to Berwick-upon-Tweed.
16 February 1963

Left above, St Margarets depot in Edinburgh served as the final store for several small tank locomotives formerly used in the area for shunting duties but ousted by diesels. This ex-NBR 'Y9' 0-4-0 saddle tank No. 68095 had not seen steam for a while. The class was introduced in 1882 to a design by Holmes and this engine has now been preserved, although not in working order, at the Bo'ness and Kinneil Railway. *Left below*, ex-CR '2P' 0-4-4 tank No. 55124 at Dalry Road depot in Edinburgh. Many ex-CR locomotives carried stovepipe chimneys but fortunately this engine retained its traditional CR style, and very handsome it looks. *Above*, on the same day at the same depot, ex-LMS class '5' 4-6-0 No. 45367 after a snow-clearing special on the line between Edinburgh and Carstairs. Once every few years there would be heavy snow falls in the central belt of Scotland and this line, with its open sections near Cobbinshaw, was particularly susceptible to drifting snow.

17 February 1963

On a crisp, bright afternoon ex-LNER 'A4' 4–6–2 No. 60016 *Silver King* sits at the head of a southbound stopping passenger train at Prestonpans station.

2 March 1963

Ex-WD '8F' 2–8–0 No. 90553 passing Portobello station having worked laboriously up the steep grade from Craigentinny goods yard with a mixed freight. The train was probably heading for the new Millerhill marshalling yard which sat abreast the Waverley route to Carlisle on the outskirts of Edinburgh. These locomotives were purchased by British Railways in 1948 from the Ministry of Supply, a large number of them having seen service abroad during the Second World War.

23 March 1963

An unusual regular steam working consisting of three non-corridor coaches and locomotive as a stopping train from Edinburgh Waverley to Berwick-upon-Tweed was known locally as the Berwick slow. This was a Saturday-only working that left Waverley about lunchtime with a similar working leaving Berwick mid-morning for Edinburgh, the trains normally passing each other at Longniddry. The working from Edinburgh was normally headed by an 'A4' or another Pacific and was part of a return working for a Newcastle engine. The Berwick to Edinburgh working was normally headed by a Standard '4MT' 2–6–4 tank or sometimes a 'B1' 4–6–0 running tender first. This photograph shows Standard '4MT' 2–6–4 tank No. 80006 running bunker first on the Edinburgh-bound trip nearing Portobello station, the last stop before Waverley.

23 March 1963

Ex-LMS class '5' 4–6–0 No. 45361 leaves Edinburgh Princes Street station with a train bound for Glasgow Central via the Shotts line. At this time all the Edinburgh Waverley to Glasgow Queen Street trains were served by diesel multiple units but the Princes Street to Glasgow Central services remained steam hauled up to the day Princes Street station was closed.

25 March 1963

29

Three ex-NBR tank engines at Kipps depot near Glasgow where they were in store awaiting their final removal for scrapping. *Above* is 'Y9' 0–4–0 saddle tank No. 68104 and *right* are two 'J88' 0–6–0 tanks, No. 68345 *(above)* and No. 68350 *(below)*. Note the two differing 'J88' chimney styles. These really were veteran classes, having been introduced in 1882 and 1904 respectively.

30 March 1963

Haymarket depot on the western side of Edinburgh supplied the locomotives for the express passenger trains on the East Coast route to London. Stabled here were examples of all the ex-LNER Pacifics. This photograph shows 'A3' 4–6–2 No. 60091 *Captain Cuttle* leaving the depot for Waverley station. The shed code (52B) indicates that the engine is allocated to Heaton depot.

31 March 1963

Ex-NBR 'J83' 0–6–0 tank No. 68481 in store at Bathgate depot. This locomotive had worked as one of the Edinburgh Waverley station pilots for many years.

4 May 1963

Ex-LNER 'V1' 2–6–2 tank No. 67649 lies in store at Bathgate depot. It is minus its front coupling and has an empty bunker which indicates that it is waiting removal to a scrapyard. This class of locomotive, together with its sister 'V3' class, worked the suburban traffic around both Edinburgh and Glasgow for many years.

4 May 1963

Ex-CR '2P' 0–4–4 tank No. 55269 at Perth depot. This class of locomotive had for many years worked the traffic on the branch lines of the old Caledonian Railway and were to be seen in the early 1960s, still working trains on the Ballachulish and Killin branches.

20 May 1963

Ex-LNER 'A4' 4–6–2 No. 60002 *Sir Murrough Wilson* pulls into the west end of Edinburgh Waverley station with, according to the head code, empty coaching stock.

3 June 1963

Ex-NBR 'J37' 0–6–0 No. 64570 has just shunted a parcels coach into the bay platform at Polmont station. Polmont was midway between Edinburgh and Glasgow and was a junction for Grangemouth where large amounts of freight traffic came out of the docks.

6 July 1963

Dalry Road depot in Edinburgh served the ex-LMS lines in the area spreading out from Princes Street station, and the bulk of the locomotives allocated to it at this time were ex-LMS class '5' or ex-CR 0–6–0s. On this day ex-LMS class '5' 4–6–0 No. 45245 is standing over one of the ashpits outside the shed.

7 July 1963

Ex-CR '3P' 4–4–0 No. 54502 in store at Carstairs junction depot. At the end of its useful life, it waits among other ex-CR locomotives for the call to the scrapyard. Designed by Pickersgill and introduced in 1920, many of these locomotives had until the late 1950s been working express passenger trains from Perth to Inverness and the north, usually in pairs to cope with the heavy trains and severe gradients.

13 July 1963

Strawfrank water troughs lay a mile or so south of Carstairs junction on the West Coast main line and was a wonderful site for photographing or simply watching traffic at the start and end of the Glasgow Trades holidays. On the first Saturday of the trades a constant stream of both regular and special trains ran south from Glasgow to the main holiday centres in England, the Lancashire coast resorts and North Wales being favourites. *Left*, ex-LMS class '5' 4–6–0 No. 44786 picks up speed after leaving Carstairs junction heading south. *Above*, Standard '7P6F' 'Britannia' 4–6–2 No. 70044 *Earl Haig* also heads south with a passenger train.

13 July 1963

On the south-eastern side of Edinburgh, Niddrie brick works lay between the city suburban line and Woolmet pit. The brick works and pit were served by a line run by the National Coal Board; coal was brought from Woolmet pit and also the nearby Niddrie pit into sidings at Niddrie west junction. This photograph shows NCB 0–6–0 saddle tank No. 25 of the Lothians Northern Area posing after having shunted a rake of wagons into the brick works. This engine was built by Andrew Barclay in 1954 and is now preserved and working at the Scottish Industrial Railway Centre at Dalmellington.

16 July 1963

On the same day as the previous photograph, NCB 0–6–0 saddle tank No. 23 is shunting wagons at
Niddrie brick works.

Standard '5MT' 4–6–0 No. 73146 sits quietly on Dalry Road depot in Edinburgh. The photograph shows clearly the Caprotti valve gear fitted to this locomotive, the engine being one of a batch of thirty introduced in 1956 fitted with this type of gear.

20 July 1963

On the same day ex-LMS '2MT' 2–6–0 No. 46482 was at the shed. These locomotives were designed by Ivatt and introduced in 1946.

At Strawfrank troughs ex-LMS class '5' 4–6–0 No. 45016 heads a passenger working south from Glasgow.

27 July 1963

Standard '7P6F' 'Britannia' 4–6–2 No. 70044 *Earl Haig* heads south over Strawfrank water troughs with a passenger working.

27 July 1963

Left, ex-LMS class '5' 4–6–0 No. 44689 with a full head of steam makes a fine start away from Carstairs junction heading south over Strawfrank troughs. The shed code plate (12A) indicates the locomotive was allocated to Carlisle Upperby depot. *Above*, on the same day ex-LMS '7P' 'Royal Scot' 4–6–0 No. 46118 *Royal Welch Fusilier* heads south over Strawfrank troughs on a passenger working.

27 July 1963

Above, ex-LMS '6P5F' 'Jubilee' 4–6–0 No. 45742 *Connaught* takes water at Strawfrank troughs on the way north. *Right*, ex-LMS '7P' 'Royal Scot' 4–6–0 No. 46155 *The Lancer* also takes water at Strawfrank troughs on the way north. Both these engines are in a very dirty state.

27 July 1963

Traffic on the Tillynaught to Banff branch of the old Great North of Scotland Railway was steam hauled up to its closure in July 1964 and on this warm summer's day Standard '2MT' 2–6–0 No. 78054, with two coaches, has arrived at Tillynaught junction from Banff and prepares to run round the stock for the return trip. This was a typical scene on many branch lines at this time with few passengers.

27 August 1963

On the same day, having run round its train, Standard '2MT' 2–6–0 No. 78054 makes the return trip to Banff. This photograph was taken on the footplate as the train left Ladysbridge station for Banff.

Ex-LMS class '5' 4–6–0 No. 44953 leaves Edinburgh Princes Street station on a passenger train to Carstairs junction.

5 October 1963

Above, ex-NBR 'J37' 0–6–0 No. 64614 reverses into Slateford yard in Edinburgh with a guard's van on 14 December 1963. This class was introduced in 1914; compare it with the more graceful ex-NBR 'J36' 0–6–0 No. 65243 *Maude* in the photograph *below*, taken at Dalry Road depot on 25 December 1963. Built in 1891, *Maude* served with the British forces in France during the First World War and was withdrawn in 1966. Fortunately it went on to be preserved and now works on the Scottish Railway Preservation Society line at Bo'ness near Falkirk.

Ex-LMS class '5' 4–6–0 No. 45127, on a very wet day, makes a slippery start away from Murrayfield station in Edinburgh with empty coaching stock. It had earlier worked a rugby supporters' special from Princes Street station. Note the wrong line working.

4 January 1964

Ex-LMS class '5' 4–6–0 No. 45478 passing Dumfries depot.

28 January 1964

Ex-CR '3F' 0–6–0 No. 57600 lying in store at Dumfries depot.

28 January 1964

Ex-LMS '2P' 4–4–0 No. 40670 in store at Dumfries depot. Although its shed code plate has disappeared, its previous allocation is clearly painted on the front buffer beam – Ayr.

28 January 1964

Late at night on the same day ex-LMS class '5' 4–6–0 No. 45126 stands in Dumfries station at the head of a train for Carlisle. This photograph clearly shows the AWS visual warning instrument and also the very grimy state of the locomotive.

Early in the morning, at the head of a rugby supporters' special, Standard '7P6F' 'Britannia' 4–6–2 No. 70025 *Western Star* waits to leave Crewe station on the last leg of the working from Edinburgh to Cardiff.

1 February 1964

On the return trip from Cardiff on the same rugby supporters' special, the last section from Carlisle to Edinburgh is worked by ex-LNER 'A1' 4–6–2 No. 60152 *Holyrood*. The locomotive is making a very slippery start away from Galashiels station.

2 February 1964

Ex-LNER 'V2' 2–6–2 No. 60813 leaves Edinburgh Waverley as a light engine heading for Haymarket depot on the western side of the city. This locomotive has a short stovepipe chimney and smoke deflectors fitted, the only one of its class to have this variation. The photograph also shows the wonderful North British Hotel which served Waverley station. The hotel was closed for almost eighteen months and completely refurbished in the early 1990s.

4 February 1964

Standard '4MT' 2–6–4 tank No. 80022 in Dalry Road depot, Edinburgh.

27 February 1964

Ex-LMS class '5' 4–6–0 No. 45053 has just been given a good going over by two young cleaners at Dalry Road in Edinburgh. Even at this late stage, only four years away from the last British Railways steam working in the UK and less than two years away from the closure of the depot, some locomotive depots and men still took a pride in their work and the stock. The shed code plate (64C) shows that this locomotive is at its home depot.

27 February 1964

A very leaky Standard '7P6F' 'Britannia' 4–6–2 No. 70036 *Boadicea* lifts a heavy passenger train away from Stirling station heading to Perth and the north.

29 February 1964

Ex-LMS class '5' 4–6–0 No. 44960 approaches Stirling station working hard on a passenger train heading to Glasgow. This locomotive is fitted with automatic tablet exchange equipment on its cab side.

29 February 1964

On the same day ex-LMS '7P' 'Patriot' 4–6–0 No. 45527 *Southport* leaves Stirling heading a northbound train, probably to Perth. This is another Carlisle Upperby (12A) locomotive and was one of the Ivatt rebuilds of the Fowler 1933 introduced '6P5F' locomotives that had previously been a rebuild of the LNWR 'Claughton' class.

Ex-LMS class '5' 4–6–0 No. 45115 waits to leave Stirling station late at night on a northbound passenger train. The shed code plate (65B) indicates that this is a St Rollox engine.

29 February 1964

On a very wet day ex-LMS '4MT' 2–6–4 tank No. 42691 waits to take empty coaching stock out of Edinburgh Waverley station to Craigentinny sidings. This was one of the Fairburn versions of this class of locomotive.

3 March 1964

Set against the massive bulk of Calton Hill, ex-LNER 'V2' 2–6–2 No. 60813 moves through Waverley station heading for St Margarets depot. This locomotive was the only one of its class to be fitted with a stovepipe chimney.

7 March 1964

Ex-LNER 'A1' 4–6–2 No. 60129 *Guy Mannering* leaves Edinburgh Waverley station heading for Haymarket depot, showing the well-proportioned front end of these locomotives.

17 March 1964

Above, ex-LMS class '5' 4–6–0 No. 44702 waits at the head of a passenger train at the western end of Edinburgh Waverley station.

17 March 1964

Right, ex-LNER 'A1' 4–6–2 No. 60152 *Holyrood* waits at the head of a passenger train in Waverley station, Edinburgh. Again, the well-proportioned front end of this class and the head of the third cylinder are clearly shown. The shed code plate (64A) indicates that the locomotive was allocated to St Margarets depot, Edinburgh.

21 March 1964

Motherwell station was on the main West Coast route to London, but very few of the expresses stopped there. It was, however, well served by local and semi–fast passenger trains. Here, Standard '7P6F' 'Britannia' 4–6–2 No. 70006 *Robert Burns* waits to pull away from the station with a passenger train.

27 March 1964

Ex-LMS class '5' 'Crab' 2–6–0 No. 42737 in a very clean condition at Corkerhill depot in Glasgow. This locomotive was allocated to Ayr (67C) depot.

27 March 1964

Corkerhill depot in Glasgow served St Enoch station and the network of old Glasgow and South Western Railway lines spreading out from there. On this day a very clean Standard '4MT' 2–6–4 tank No. 80047 simmers quietly outside the shed. The shed code plate indicates that it is at its home depot (67A). The staff at this depot must have taken a great deal of pride in the locomotives as even at this time most of the stock was kept in a very clean condition.

27 March 1964

Ex-LMS '7P' 'Royal Scot' 4–6–0 No. 46166 *London Rifle Brigade* sitting over the ashpits at Polmadie depot, Glasgow. This locomotive was allocated to Carlisle Upperby (12A) depot.

27 March 1964

Ex-LNER 'A2' 4–6–2 No. 60535 *Hornet's Beauty* at Polmadie depot, Glasgow. This engine was one of the A.H. Peppercorn 1947 developments of the Thompson 'A2/2' locomotives.

27 March 1964

Ex-LMS '8P' 'Coronation' 4–6–2 No. 46237 *City of Bristol* backs out of Glasgow Central station heading for Polmadie depot. The engine had earlier arrived with an express passenger train from London.

27 March 1964

A stranger to Edinburgh, ex-LMS '8P' 'Coronation' 4–6–2 No. 46256 *Sir William A. Stanier F.R.S.*, has worked an enthusiasts' special into the city and is being coaled up at St Margarets depot before resting overnight. The engine was allocated to Crewe North (5A) depot and was one of two locomotives in the class introduced by H.G. Ivatt ten years after the original Stanier design.

29 March 1964

Having been coaled up, No. 46256 is being squeezed on to the turntable at St Margarets depot for turning before its overnight stop in the city.

Ex-LMS 7P 'Royal Scot' 4–6–0 No. 46162 *Queen's Westminster Rifleman* at Polmadie depot, Glasgow. Yet another Carlisle Upperby (12A) locomotive.

11 April 1964

Ex-LMS class '5' 4–6–0 No. 44721 drifts slowly through Aberdeen station with a freight train which was probably destined for Kittybrewster yard on the northern side of the city.

18 April 1964

Ex-WD '8F' 2–8–0 No. 90705 moves slowly towards the coaling shed in Aberdeen Ferryhill depot.
18 April 1964

Ex-LMS class '5' 4–6–0 No. 44721 makes a very lively start passing Ferryhill depot in Aberdeen with a passenger train heading south for Glasgow.

18 April 1964

Ex-LNER 'V2' 2–6–2 No. 60846 accelerates south from Aberdeen past Ferryhill depot, heading a passenger train.

18 April 1964

Ex-LNER 'A4' 4–6–2 No. 60009 *Union of South Africa* waits at the foot of the Calton tunnel in Edinburgh while the driver telephones for instructions. The locomotive is in a gleaming condition ready to haul an enthusiasts' special south. This locomotive has been successfully preserved and has headed many specials throughout the British Isles.

9 May 1964

Ex-LMS class '5' 4–6–0 No. 44986 rests at Dumfries station on a freight train heading south to Carlisle.

16 May 1964

Ex-LMS class '5' 'Crab' 2–6–0 No. 42739 rests in Dumfries shed. Although awkward in appearance, these were powerful locomotives used on freight workings throughout ex-LMS territory.

16 May 1964

The driver takes the tablet from the signalman at Castle Douglas signal-box as Standard '4MT' 2–6–4 tank No. 80076 heads down the single line branch to Kirkcudbright.

16 May 1964

On the same day Standard '4MT' tank No. 80076 has just arrived at Kirkcudbright from Dumfries on the branch from Castle Douglas. The group of gentlemen on the platform are awaiting the unloading of racing pigeon baskets, still a regular traffic throughout most regions at this time. Within a year this branch was closed.

Standard '4MT' 2–6–4 tank No. 80076 is seen here in Kirkcudbright station yard running round the train it has just brought from Castle Douglas.

16 May 1964

Ex-LNER 'B1' 4–6–0 No. 61357 sits quietly on its home depot (64A) St Margarets, Edinburgh. The depot was allocated a number of this class, which at this time were regularly used on freight and empty coaching stock workings between Craigentinny carriage sidings and Waverley station. The electric lamps on the front buffer beam and on top of the smokebox were fitted to a number of this class of engine.

20 May 1964

Above, ex-LNER 'A1' 4–6–2 No. 60140 *Balmoral* enters Edinburgh Waverley station with a passenger train from Carlisle and the south. *Right*, having worked into the Waverley station from Carlisle, No. 60140 *Balmoral* bursts from The Mound tunnel heading the empty coaching stock for the yard.

30 May 1964

Ex-LNER 'A4' 4–6–2 No. 60004 *William Whitelaw* simmers quietly outside St Margarets shed in Edinburgh. As Haymarket shed, on the western side of Edinburgh, became the main depot for diesel locomotives working out of Edinburgh, St Margarets seemed to become busier with steam locomotives.

2 June 1964

Ex-LNER 'A4' 4–6–2 No. 60034 *Lord Faringdon* in a very grimy state has reversed into St Margarets depot in Edinburgh and is sitting over one of the ashpits.

6 June 1964

St Boswells station on the Waverley route was the junction for the cross-country, cross-border line to Kelso, Coldstream and Berwick-upon-Tweed. On this day Standard class '4MT' 2–6–0 No. 76050 is taking water before starting its journey to Berwick, two days before the closure of the line to passenger traffic.

13 June 1964

Somewhat of a rarity, one of only ten built, Standard '6P5F' 'Clan' 4–6–2 No. 72008 *Clan Macleod* breasts Beattock Summit in fine style with a six-coach passenger train heading north.

20 June 1964

A sad sight at Carlisle Upperby depot, ex-LMS '8P' 'Princess' 4–6–2 No. 46200 *The Princess Royal* sits in store awaiting its fate, which unfortunately was the scrapyard. One of a pair introduced in 1933, its sister engine No. 46201 *Princess Elizabeth* was lucky enough to be preserved and is based at the Bulmer Railway Centre.

20 June 1964

Ex-LMS '7P' 'Patriot' 4–6–0 No. 45532 *Illustrious* in store with its coupling rods removed at Carlisle Upperby depot.

20 June 1964

Ex-LMS '4MT' 2–6–4 tank No. 42198 at Kendal station on a train heading for Windermere. This was one of the Fairburn developments of a Stanier design. The shed code plate (10A) indicates that this engine was allocated to Spring Branch.

20 June 1964

On this bright day ex-LMS '4MT' 2–6–4 tank No. 42240 waits to leave Birkenhead (Woodside) on a stopping train to Chester. The shed code plate (6A) indicates that this engine was allocated to Chester Midland.

21 June 1964

Chester Midland depot, Standard class '4MT' 4–6–0 No. 75027 coals up from an antiquated coaling conveyor. The shed code plate (6C) tells us that the locomotive was allocated to Birkenhead depot. This locomotive was lucky enough to be preserved and is now based at the Bluebell Railway.

21 June 1964

This ex-LMS '8F' 2–8–0 No. 48171 looks in very clean condition as it moves into Chester Midland depot for coaling. Only a very few examples of this once-numerous class have been preserved.

21 June 1964

Chester Midland depot stabled a wide variety of engines; those on shed on this day included ex-GWR '6800' class 'Grange' 4–6–0 No. 6861 *Crynant Grange*.

21 June 1964

Standard class '4MT' 4–6–0 No. 75006 at Chester Midland depot. This was one of the few in this class introduced in 1957 to be fitted with a double chimney, and was allocated to Birkenhead (6C) depot.

21 June 1964

Ex-GWR '5700' class 0–6–0 pannier tank No. 3754 in very clean condition at Shrewsbury depot.
22 June 1964

Ex-GWR '6800' class 'Grange' 4–6–0 No. 6826 *Nannerth Grange* pulls a train of coal wagons through Gloucester East station.

22 June 1964

Ex-GWR '1400' class 0–4–2 tank No. 1444 simmers gently at Gloucester (Barnwood) depot. Fortunately four engines from this class, introduced in 1932, have been preserved.

22 June 1964

Ex-GWR '4900' class 'Hall' 4–6–0 No. 6936 *Breccles Hall* pauses in Exeter Central station at the head of a passenger train. Several of this class have also been preserved.

25 June 1964

Exeter Central station was the resting place for iron ore trains that had made the steep climb up from St David's station. This photograph shows Standard '4MT' 2–6–4 tank No. 80039 piloting ex-SR '7P5F' 'West Country' 4–6–2 No. 34099 *Lynmouth* into Central station. There would also be bankers at the rear of the train which would detach at Central station.

25 June 1964

On the same day ex-SR '7P5F' 'Battle of Britain' 4–6–2 No. 34057 *Biggin Hill* sits in Exeter Central station at the head of an ore train that it has just pulled up the bank from St David's station.

Ex-LMS '2MT' 2–6–2 tank No. 41224 running bunker first on a passenger train near Fremington on the line between Barnstaple and Bideford. This engine was one of the H.G. Ivatt designs introduced in 1946.

26 June 1964

Ex-LMS '2MT' 2–6–2 tank No. 41290 at Barnstaple depot. Four of this class of locomotive have been preserved.

26 June 1964

Ex-LMS '2MT' 2–6–2 tank No. 41224 pauses in Bideford station with a passenger train.

26 June 1964

Wadebridge yard shunter ex-GWR '1366' class 0–6–0 pannier tank No. 1367. One of this diminutive class of pannier tanks has been preserved, No. 1369, based at the South Devon Railway.

27 June 1964

Ex-GWR '2884' class 2–8–0 No. 3836 at Mold junction depot. A number of these powerful locomotives have been preserved.

2 July 1964

Standard '4MT' 2–6–4 tank No. 80026 at St Margarets depot in Edinburgh.

5 July 1964

Ex-LNER 'A3' 4–6–2 No. 60051 *Blink Bonny* reverses into Edinburgh Waverley station prior to heading a train to the north.

13 July 1964

Standard '7P6F' 'Britannia' 4–6–2 No. 70038 *Robin Hood* takes water on board as it heads north over Strawfrank troughs. These troughs were well used by locomotives heading north to Glasgow but particularly by those heading non-stop to Stirling and Perth with trains for the north of Scotland.

18 July 1964

Ex-LNER 'A4' 4–6–2 No. 60010 *Dominion of Canada* in a very grimy state at St Margarets depot, Edinburgh. This locomotive was lucky enough to be preserved, but in Canada.

19 July 1964

Princes Street station in Edinburgh was served almost exclusively by ex-LMS locomotives right up to its closure. It was therefore a rarity to see ex-LNER 'B1' 4–6–0 No. 61134 heading out on a passenger working.

13 August 1964

The branch from Thornton junction to Crail wandered up the Fife coast of the Firth of Forth and served some beautiful fishing villages with one goods train per day and a few passenger trains. On this day we have a driver's view approaching Anstruther on the footplate of ex-LNER 'B1' 4–6–0 No. 61103 heading for Thornton junction on the afternoon passenger train.

19 September 1964

The same train has arrived at Cameron Bridge and waits to leave for Thornton. Cameron Bridge is still famous for its distillery which produces the only single grain whisky to be bottled and sold to the public.

19 September 1964

Ex-LNER 'B1' 4–6–0 No. 61103 is seen here at Crail station waiting to return to Thornton junction on an afternoon passenger train. This duty normally consisted of bringing up the train in the morning, waiting a couple of hours and returning in the afternoon. The shed code plate (62A) indicates that the locomotive was allocated to Thornton. This line was closed almost a year later in September 1965.

21 September 1964

Ex-LNER 'A4' 4–6–2 No. 60009 *Union of South Africa*, in very clean condition, waits at Niddrie West junction to take over a special enthusiasts' train working. This locomotive was preserved privately and has worked many successful specials.

26 September 1964

Left, Aberdeen gasworks was reached by rail from the old Waterloo yard along Waterloo and Regent Quays in the harbour. Gasworks 0–4–0 saddle tank No. 3 makes its way to Waterloo yard to bring some oil wagons back to the gasworks. *Above*, on the same day No. 3 waits in Waterloo yard before running back along the quays with its train of oil wagons. This beautiful little engine was built by Andrew Barclay in 1926 and is still in existence, although not in working order.

17 October 1964

Ex-LNER 'A3' 4–6–2 No. 60100 *Spearmint* sits over the ashpits at St Margarets depot in Edinburgh. It has been cleaned in preparation for a special working south. The stripe on the cab side indicates that the locomotive was not allowed to work over lines fitted with overhead electric cables.

31 October 1964

Midcalder junction is in the middle of nowhere, about a 2-mile walk from the station of the same name. It is the point where the line from Edinburgh Princes Street splits for Carstairs junction and Glasgow via Shotts. This photograph shows ex-LMS class '5' 4–6–0 No. 45127 lifting a train of full coal wagons from the Glasgow line into the yard at Midcalder junction.

7 November 1964

Standard '7P6F' 'Britannia' 4–6–2 No. 70013 *Oliver Cromwell* passes Midcalder junction with a freight train from Edinburgh heading south to Carstairs. This locomotive was the last surviving 'Britannia' to work on British Railways and served right up to the last days in August 1968. It was lucky enough to be preserved and can be seen at the Bressingham Steam Museum.

7 November 1964

Ex-LNER 'B1' 4–6–0 No. 61029 *Chamois* sits over the ashpits at St Margarets depot, Edinburgh. This was one of a number of this class of locomotive to be allocated within the Edinburgh area.

23 January 1965

Ex-LNER 'V2' 2–6–2 No. 60855 on St Margarets shed, Edinburgh. This photograph shows the excellent proportions and graceful lines of the front end of this Gresley-designed locomotive.

23 January 1965

With the impending closure of Dalry Road depot in Edinburgh, more ex-LMS locomotives were stabled at St Margarets depot. Here ex-LMS '2MT' 2–6–0 No. 46462 sits over the ashpits bearing the shed code (64A) for St Margarets.

27 March 1965

Standard '4MT' 2–6–0 No. 76050 sits on the coaling line at St Margarets depot, Edinburgh. The full tubs of coal are ready for loading. All the work of coaling was done manually at this depot.

27 March 1965

Two ex-LNER 'B1' 4–6–0 locomotives at St Margarets depot in Edinburgh; No. 61404 stands behind No. 61354.

27 March 1965

Ex-LNER 'V2' 2–6–2 No. 60846 sits over the ashpits at St Margarets depot, Edinburgh.

4 April 1965

Ex-LNER 'B1' 4–6–0 No. 61345 reverses slowly from the ashpits at St Margarets depot prior to going into the shed.

4 April 1965

Ex-LMS class '5' 4–6–0 No. 44704 drifts into Forfar station as a light engine heading south. The shed code plate (63A) and front buffer beam tell us that this locomotive was allocated to Perth.

24 April 1965

A very clean ex-LMS class '5' 4–6–0 No. 44998 in gleaming condition waits at Aberdeen to take empty coaching stock to the yard. This locomotive has probably just come from Inverurie works after being overhauled. The shed code plate (63A) indicates that this engine was also allocated to Perth.

24 April 1965

Ex-LMS class '5' 4–6–0 No. 44998 again sits at the head of empty coaching stock in Aberdeen waiting for the off to the yard. This photograph shows the graceful strength of the motion which drove these locomotives.

26 April 1965

The Waverley route between Edinburgh and Carlisle handled large amounts of freight traffic. Here, ex-LNER 'A3' 4–6–2 No. 60041 *Salmon Trout* heads north on a freight train approaching Galashiels.
17 May 1965

Ex-LNER 'A3' 4–6–2 No. 60052 *Prince Palatine* in very clean condition at St Margarets in Edinburgh, waiting to leave the depot to head up a special train. The diagonal stripe on the cab side indicates that the locomotive was not allowed to run over lines fitted with overhead electric cables.

29 May 1965

Ex-LNER 'B1' 4–6–0 No. 61180 sits over the ashpits at St Margarets depot in Edinburgh.

29 May 1965

Ex-LMS class '5' 4–6–0 No. 45477 sits quietly (*above and right*) at the entrance to Dalry Road depot in Edinburgh. The shed code plate (64C) and front buffer beam confirm that it is at its home depot. This depot was closed within a couple of months of these photographs being taken.

16 July 1965

Ex-LNER 'A4' 4–6–2 No. 60007 *Sir Nigel Gresley* reverses on to a train at Edinburgh Waverley station which is bound for Dundee and Aberdeen. At this time most of the passenger trains to Aberdeen were hauled by diesel locomotives, but the occasional working would be steam hauled. This locomotive went on to be preserved and has worked many enthusiasts' specials.

17 July 1965

Ex-LNER 'A2' 4–6–2 No. 60532 *Blue Peter* lifts a freight train away from Dundee Tay Bridge yard heading north for Aberdeen. The photograph was taken from a passing train heading south. This locomotive has also been preserved and is based at the North Yorkshire Moors Railway.

17 July 1965

Another rarity, a Standard '5MT' 4–6–0 No. 73152 fitted with Caprotti valve gear, in Dundee Tay Bridge depot. Although it has no shed code plate, the front buffer beam tells us that its home depot is, or was, St Rollox, Glasgow.

17 July 1965

Ex-NBR 'J36' 0–6–0 No. 65319, which has a tender with a tender cab fitted, at Dundee Tay Bridge depot.

17 July 1965

Ex-LNER 'A2' 4–6–2 No. 60528 *Tudor Minstrel* sits quietly outside the shed at Dundee Tay Bridge depot, giving some impression of the size of the firebox on these locomotives.

17 July 1965

Ex-LMS class '5' 4–6–0 No. 45084 pauses at Stirling station with a passenger train, probably from Glasgow to Perth. The shed code plate (65J) indicates that the locomotive is allocated to Stirling depot.

17 July 1965

Detail of the front motion on Standard '4MT' 2–6–4 tank No. 80113 at St Margarets depot, Edinburgh.

17 May 1966

Ex-LMS class '5' 4–6–0 No. 45053 on the ashpits at St Margarets depot, Edinburgh.

8 July 1966